C000054900

Peak
District

Compiled by
Kevin Borman

JARROLD

 Mapping sourced from Ordnance Survey®

Acknowledgements

I am very grateful to the following people, who have made the job of writing and illustrating this guidebook easier, more accurate and more enjoyable. Terry Marsh of the Outdoor Writers' Guild kindly suggested my name to the publishers, where Sarah Letts has proved a most supportive editor. Roly Smith, also of the Outdoor Writers' Guild, has for many years encouraged me in my writings about the Peak District. Jeff Winston and Alison Foster of the Peak District National Park Authority were very efficient in responding to my queries. Phil Hardy, with whom I've walked many a hill, cast an experienced eye over the text and made several helpful suggestions. Finally, thanks to my partner Troy Roberts. Walking in the Peak District with her continues to be a delight. She has made thorough and constructive comments on the text, and shown understanding beyond the call of duty while I have been chained to the word processor for hours on end.

Text:	Kevin Borman
Photography:	Kevin Borman
Editor:	Sarah Letts
Designer:	Doug Whitworth

OS Ordnance Survey This product includes mapping data licensed from Ordnance Survey ® with the permission of the Controller of Her Majesty's Stationery Office. © Crown Copyright 2001. All rights reserved. Licence number 100017593. Pathfinder is a registered trade mark of Ordnance Survey, the national mapping agency of Great Britain.

Jarrold Publishing ISBN 0-7117-1603-X

While every care has been taken to ensure the accuracy of the route directions, the publishers cannot accept responsibility for errors or omissions, or for changes in details given. The countryside is not static: hedges and fences can be removed, field boundaries can alter, footpaths can be rerouted and changes in ownership can result in the closure or diversion of some concessionary paths. Also, paths that are easy and pleasant for walking in fine conditions may become slippery, muddy and difficult in wet weather, while stepping-stones across rivers and streams may become impassable.

If you find an inaccuracy in either the text or maps, please write or e-mail to Jarrold Publishing at the addresses below.

First published 2001 by Jarrold Publishing

Printed in Belgium
by Proost NV, Turnhout. 1/01

Jarrold Publishing
Pathfinder Guides, Whitefriars,
Norwich NR3 1TR
E-mail: pathfinder@jarrold.com
www.jarrold-publishing.co.uk/pathfinders

Front cover: Plateau scenery above Monk's Dale
Previous page: Birchen Edge

Contents

Keymap

Introduction

The routes and information in this book have been devised specifically with families and children in mind. All the walks include points of interest and most include a question to provide an objective.

If you, or your children, have not walked before, choose from the shorter walks for your first outings. The purpose is not simply to get from A to B but to enjoy an exploration, which may be just a steady stroll in the countryside.

The walks are graded by length and difficulty, but few landscapes are truly flat, so even shorter walks may involve some ascent. Details are given under Route Features in the first information box for each route. But the precise nature of the ground underfoot will depend on recent weather conditions. If you do set out on a walk and discover the going is harder than you expected, or the weather has deteriorated, do not be afraid to turn back. The route will always be there another day, when you are fitter or the children are more experienced or the weather is better.

Bear in mind that the countryside also changes. Landmarks may disappear, gates may become stiles, rights of way may be altered. However, with the aid of this book and its maps you should be able to enjoy many interesting family walks in the countryside.

All the walks included are within the Peak District National Park. They have been chosen to provide a good geographical spread, they are all of modest length and all have several points of interest.

As explained below, the Peak District receives many visitors. However, most of them tend not to set foot outside the 'honeypot' villages such as Ashford in the Water, Hathersage and Eyam. On even a short walk, you will leave most of the crowds behind and the satisfaction of discovering the landscape at a slow pace will make for a memorable outing. Sampling a few of these walks among the striking scenery of the Peak District should soon make you realise why the area is so popular.

The Peak District National Park

Those who do not know the Peak District might assume that the name refers to a region of pointed mountains. Whilst there are a few shapely summits in the area, the highest land is actually to be found on the almost flat plateaux in the north.

Errwood and Fernilee reservoirs from Goyt Valley

The area was first called Peac-land by the Anglo-Saxons, the local tribe being the Pecsaetan, meaning 'peak-dwellers'. The word most probably comes from the Old English peac, meaning 'hill', though the area is one of varied upland scenery rather than distinct individual hills. Nowadays it is often colloquially referred to as 'the Peak', and sometimes quite incorrectly as 'the Peaks'.

The Peak Park is managed by a Joint Planning Board, which has the tricky job of reconciling the interests of the Park's 40,000 or so residents and those of its millions of visitors. Large areas of the Peak Park belong to the water companies and the National Trust, with a patchwork of smaller holdings owned by the National Park Authority, conservation bodies, forestry interests, quarry companies, private landowners, individual farmers and so on. Both the land itself and the visitors who are attracted by the land are sources of income for the residents of the Park.

Dark Peak and White Peak

The Peak District is sub-divided, on the basis of its contrasting scenery, into the White Peak and the Dark Peak, and these names are used on the two Ordnance Survey maps which cover the Peak District. The names derive from the distinctive geology of the area.

Dark Peak refers to those areas with gritstone bedrock. Gritstone is a kind of sandstone which, when exposed, weathers to a very dark brown, almost black colour. This rock forms the basis of the northern part of the Peak District, but also extends southwards along the eastern and western sides, forming a kind of horseshoe, albeit with a very broad arch at the top. In the north it gives rise to the high, open moorland of Kinder Scout, Bleaklow and Black Hill.

These moors have an elemental character, combining areas of peat the colour of plain chocolate, with expanses of heather, bilberry and cotton grass. Resistant rocky tors, eroded by the weather into remarkable shapes in some places, dot the empty, brooding moors of the Dark Peak, the territory of red grouse, mountain hare and sheep.

In a number of the Dark Peak valleys, reservoirs have been constructed, adding a further dimension to this landscape which, whilst it may look untamed, has to a large extent been shaped by human activities.

The eastern and western arms of the Dark Peak have a less wild feel, with the remains of an eroded dome of gritstone having left distinctive crags, the 'edges' which have become a favourite haunt of rock climbers. These are more prominent in the east than the west, with Stanage Edge perhaps the best known of all.

The southern part of the Peak District is formed of greyish white Carboniferous limestone, hence the name White Peak. The limestone

Drystone wall, near Wetton

originally lay beneath a gritstone dome. Erosion of the gritstone aeons ago has revealed the pale limestone, which now forms a high plateau of green fields deeply dissected by the valleys of several attractive rivers such as the Lathkill and the Dove. Drystone walls, steep crags, underground caverns and narrow pinnacles also characterise the White Peak.

Wellington Monument, Baslow Edge

Note: Walk 1 The passage of the Transport Act, which occurred during the preparation of this book, allows local authorities to charge a toll on roads in specific circumstances. It is expected that Derbyshire County Council will charge a toll on the minor road leading north from the A57 to Fairholmes at peak times, such as Sundays and Bank Holidays throughout the year, plus Saturdays from Easter to the end of October. The toll would be run in conjunction with car parking charges at Fairholmes. The precise level of charges is expected to be roughly equivalent to the cost of all day parking in a High Peak or Derbyshire Dales local authority car park. Additional bus services will also run at these times. The earliest that such a scheme is likely to begin operating is October 2001 and it may well be delayed beyond that. At the time of writing final details of this scheme remained to be decided. This toll, if instituted, will have an impact on drivers heading for Walk 1, which begins at Fairholmes, so this would be a good walk to choose for a quieter time of the week or the year.

Note: Walk 18 Access for drivers to the starting point of this walk in the Goyt Valley is also subject to a traffic management scheme, this one being of long standing. Access to the car park where the walk begins is available at all times via The Street from Pym Chair and via Goyt's Lane from the east. However, the road south from Errwood Reservoir via Goyt's Clough to Derbyshire Bridge is closed to all traffic on Sundays and Bank Holidays from May to September. At other times this road is one-way only in a north to south direction.

1 *Fairholmes and a Sheepdog's Memorial*

START	Fairholmes
DISTANCE	1¼ miles (2km)
TIME	1 hour
PARKING	Fairholmes (pay and display)
ROUTE FEATURES	A very gentle walk. A moderate initial incline, then downhill or level on easy paths

This, the easiest route in the book, is ideal for parents with young children who have not walked in the countryside before. It is a gentle circuit through woodland and on a path alongside a reservoir, with plenty of incidental interest, including a memorial to a faithful sheepdog, fine views and a modern totem pole.

🖉 Start at the exit to the Fairholmes car park. Cross the road and go through the gate marked 'Forest Walk to Locker-brook and Derwent Discovery Walk'. The path climbs easily into deciduous woodland, with a stream initially close by on the left.

Ⓐ After 400 yds (365m) the path reaches a bridge over an artificial water conduit. Cross this and turn right at a finger-post marked 'Concession Footpath Derwent Reservoir'. A low wooden post with a red waymark indicates the way along a well-surfaced path. After a gentle rise, the path eases downhill with the water channel nearby on the right.

After 300 yds (274m), the path passes into an area of unusual trees. These are Western Red Cedars, whose leaves have an attractive smell when crushed. The path leads on to a broad forest road, which continues in a northerly

PUBLIC TRANSPORT Buses from Manchester, Sheffield and Bakewell. Enquiry line tel. 0870 6082608. *Note:* At the time of writing the possibility of road tolls on the minor road along the Derwent Valley to Fairholmes is being discussed. See the note for Walk 1 on page 9.
REFRESHMENTS Kiosk and picnic tables at Fairholmes
PUBLIC TOILETS Fairholmes
CHILDREN'S PLAY AREA Adjoining car park
ORDNANCE SURVEY MAP Outdoor Leisure 1 (The Peak District – Dark Peak area)

direction. Beyond a gate and a red and white pole barrier, the track reaches a minor road where a stream tumbles down from Ashton Clough on the left.

B Turn right at the road, avoiding the cattle-grid by using the gate. Follow the elevated path, which provides excellent views across the Derwent Reservoir. On the left is a memorial to a heroic local sheepdog who stayed by the body of her dead master, Joseph Tagg, on Howden Moors for fifteen weeks

Derwent Dam overspill just north of Fairholmes

during the winter of 1953–4. The memorial was paid for by public subscription.

? **What was the name of the loyal sheepdog commemorated here?**

After 20 yds (18m) there is a view-point with information panels. Close by, at the entrance to Derwent Dam, is a memorial to the 'Dambusters' of 617 Squadron who practised low-level night flying here during World War II. On occasions a small museum of Dambusters memorabilia is open in the gatehouse of Derwent Dam.

Just beyond the small parking area by the dam, a footpath goes off to the left, down some steps. There are good views of the dam wall from here. Continue along to a surfaced road, turning sharp left onto it.

C For a close-up view of the dam wall, simply continue along the tarmac road, and then bear left across the open, grassy area below the dam. Return to the tarmac and retrace your steps then, just before the point where you first came onto the road, a footpath on the left leads the final few yards back to Fairholmes.

By the café at Fairholmes is the Upper Derwent Bio-Diversity Pole. Look carefully and you can find a badger, goshawk, heron and curlew among the carvings on the pole. ●

Bio-Diversity Pole at Fairholmes

Caverns and Landslips near Castleton

START Winnats
DISTANCE 2½ miles (4km)
TIME 2 hours
PARKING Winnats Pass &
Speedwell Cavern long
stay car park (pay and
display). Accessed by right
fork on the main road west
out of Castleton
ROUTE FEATURES Field
paths and a landslipped
road. Can be muddy and
slippery after rain.
Significant ascent on first
half of route. Dogs must
be kept on a lead

2

This walk begins west of Castleton, at the base of Winnats. After visiting the entrances to three limestone caverns, it reaches the ruins of the old A625 below the crumbling face of Mam Tor. The route then descends to Odin Mine, with its nearby crushing circle. A level final section completes the circuit.

From the top of the car park, take either of the squeeze stiles and cross the field to Speedwell Cavern. Go to the upper edge of the car park for a spectacular view of Winnats Pass. A narrow road twists up the valley at a gradient of 1 in 5, flanked by dramatic limestone crags.

From the car park, take the stile opposite the entrance to Speedwell Cavern. A narrow path soon begins to gain height across the hillside, before intercepting the concrete access path to Treak Cliff Cavern.

A The footpath passes behind the low buildings at the entrance to Treak Cliff Cavern then climbs north-west across the hillside, providing superb views east along the Hope Valley. After climbing to

The **show caverns** are partly naturally eroded passageways and partly the work of lead miners. On this hillside near Castleton they stumbled on a unique stained fluorspar. This came to be called Blue John and is still mined and turned into locally sold jewellery. A visit to one of the caverns, if time allows, would add an extra dimension to this walk.

PUBLIC TRANSPORT Bus connections to Edale, Castleton and beyond.
Enquiry line tel. 0870 6082608
REFRESHMENTS At Speedwell, Treak Cliff and Peak Caverns. Pubs and cafés in Castleton
PUBLIC TOILETS In Castleton. Also at the various caverns for customers
ORDNANCE SURVEY MAP Outdoor Leisure 1 (The Peak District – Dark Peak area)

a stile, the line of the path is indicated by a yellow arrow waymark.

To the north-west there is a powerful view of the exposed south-east face of Mam Tor. Beyond a grassy rise, the path dips to Blue John

The crushing circle at Odin Mine

Cavern. Continue along the short access road then, when you meet an apparently sound tarmac road, turn right and go down to the Blue John Viewpoint and information board.

B A gate beyond the traffic turning circle allows you to continue. For the ¹/₂ mile (800m), as you follow

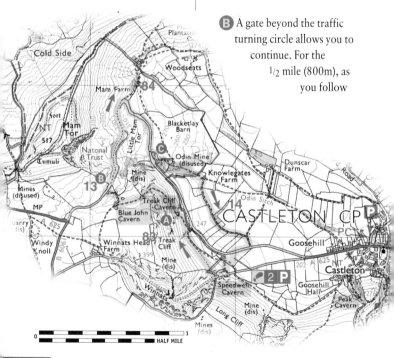

the twists of the road downhill, the power of nature is dramatically evident. The remnants of the road are cracked, warped and shattered across the hummocky terrain of a massive landslip.

By a gate where the road finally levels out again, another board gives details about the Mam Tor landslip. A little further on, a cleft in a limestone face on the right marks the site of Odin Mine, once worked for lead.

Mam Tor's geology, alternating tilted layers of shale and sandstone, is very unstable and has turned one side of the hill into a crumbling crag. In the late 1970s a major landslip destroyed the A625, then the main road between Sheffield and Chapel en le Frith.

Can you remember the names of the three caverns you have passed on this walk?

C Go through a gate on the left of the road, which leads to the easily visible crushing circle associated with the mine.

The path crosses a tiny wooden bridge beyond the crushing circle and negotiates stiles to reach Knowlegates Farm. A finger-post indicates 'Winnats' along the farm access track, which leads to a minor road. Go right here to return to the car park.

Mam Tor from Odin Mine; Lose Hill Ridge from Odin Mine

● Cave ● heather moors ● views ● gritstone edges

3 *Stanage Edge and Higger Tor*

This easy walk gives a splendid introduction to the 'heather and gritstone' landscape that characterises the Dark Peak. An airy walk along Stanage Edge, a Mecca for climbers, allows an exploration of Robin Hood's Cave. Higger Tor is an exquisite miniature plateau. Dogs must be kept on a lead.

START Upper Burbage Bridge
DISTANCE 3 miles (4.8km) Shorter version 2 miles (3.2 km)
TIME 2 hours (1½ hours for shorter version)
PARKING Upper Burbage Bridge car park (free)
ROUTE FEATURES Paths on gritstone moorland. Muddy in places, with some boulders. Several stiles

Turn left out of the car park, along the road for 50 yds (46m), to the sharp bend. Here, take the path on the right by a huge stone block. The path gently gains height as it heads west.

A Before long an optional diversion can be made to a huge boulder, the Cowper Stone, on the right. This stone is so large that it is individually named on the Ordnance Survey map. At the point where you would turn off to go to the Cowper Stone, a memorial tablet has been inset into the footpath at ground level.

Who is commemorated on this stone?

Back on the main path, pass to the left of fencing where the ground steepens, and then clamber briefly on boulders to reach the southern end of Stanage Edge. After this the path bears left and reaches flagstones. Soon the triangulation pillar, perched prominently on massive gritstone boulders, is reached.

B For the short version of the route, go north just 40 yds (37m) from the triangulation pillar, to a

PUBLIC TRANSPORT None suitable
REFRESHMENTS There is often an ice cream van at the car park in summer. Otherwise there is a good choice of cafés and pubs in Hathersage, 3 miles (4.8km) south-west
PUBLIC TOILETS None
ORDNANCE SURVEY MAP Outdoor Leisure 1 (The Peak District – Dark Peak area)

notch on the left where a narrow path leads through the boulders. (Look for point **B** in the text below to continue the route description.)

For the full route, remember this notch for future reference, but continue ahead on the crest of Stanage Edge. The path weaves among boulders,

declining gently, for 1/2 mile (800m), during which there are superb views west to Win Hill, Lose Hill, Mam Tor and Kinder Scout.

C Watch on the left for a gritty path which goes half-left, down an

Stanage Edge from Higger Tor

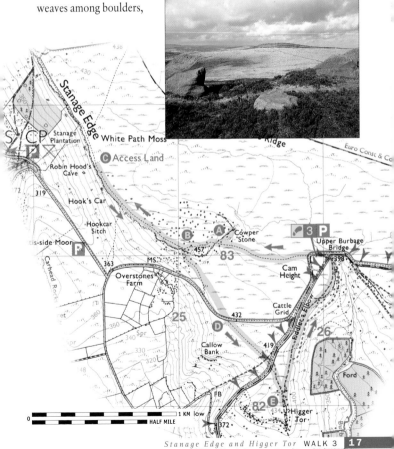

easy rocky gully, to a balcony. Erosion has honeycombed the rock into remarkable cubby-holes. Go through the furthest dark hole, bend double and you emerge in a splendid belvedere with a rocky parapet. This is Robin Hood's Cave.

In the early days of rock-climbing on Stanage Edge, climbers would use **Robin Hood's Cave** as a 'bivvy', a place to sleep overnight – free of charge, albeit hardly comfortable – and in a place where they could start climbing immediately again the following morning.

The view west from Stanage Edge

Retrace your steps to the notch just north of the triangulation pillar at point **B**. The path passing through it then goes half-left below the craggy edge.

The path becomes a well-graded, roughly surfaced track. Where it forks, with a minor road to the right, stay left, taking a grassy track that levels out to meet the road further south.

D Go over the stile opposite and bear half-left. A path leads gently downhill to a further minor road. Cross this at opposing stiles and climb the steps on the restored footpath up Higger Tor. An exploration of this small, heathery plateau is worthwhile for the many superb viewpoints it provides.

E Close to the top of the steps where you arrived on Higger Tor, a small wooden waymark with a white arrow indicates the path north. This dips, then gradually rises across the western flank of the Burbage Valley. There is a tiny, steep rise, then a final muddy section, before the path swings left to reach the car park. ●

Dovestone Reservoir

This is an easy route. An almost level circuit of Dovestone Reservoir under the edge of the Saddleworth Moors provides wonderful views of the wild slopes and tumbling crags which surround the reservoirs. Halfway along the walk there's an attractive picnic site. Dogs must be kept under close control.

START Dovestone Reservoir

DISTANCE 2½ miles (4.4km)

TIME 2 hours

PARKING Dovestone Reservoir car park. Pay and display at weekends, free at other times

ROUTE FEATURES An almost level, well-made path, which can be used by wheelchairs and push-chairs, in the direction described (anticlockwise), due to a short, steep slope near Yeoman Hey.

4

From the top end of the car park, climb the few steps, or bypass them to the right, to reach two information boards at the edge of Dovestone Reservoir. Turn right at these boards and take the tarmac lane past Dovestone Sailing Club. Dovestone Reservoir (also often spelt Dove Stone) is one of four reservoirs built in the valley where the Chew Brook and Greenfield Brook converge. Continue along the lane beyond a gate by the yacht compound.

Ⓐ Cross the bridge over the Chew Brook and go immediately left.

? *Which 'Way' is indicated on a sign at this point?*

Beyond a footbridge the path winds easily upwards past a 'Life for a Life' memorial garden on the left.

The well-surfaced path is now a little way above the level of the

PUBLIC TRANSPORT None to the reservoir. Buses from Oldham and Manchester serve Greenfield. GMPTE tel. 0161 228 7811

REFRESHMENTS Picnic tables halfway along the walk. Sandwich bar and pubs in Greenfield, 1 mile (1.6km) west

PUBLIC TOILETS Dovestone Reservoir car park

ORDNANCE SURVEY MAP Outdoor Leisure 1 (The Peak District – Dark Peak area)

reservoir. At a wooden gate with an adjacent silver birch and 'Boundary of Open Country' sign, there are fine views across the water to Alderman's Hill.

All around lies impressive scenery. Sheep graze on the lower slopes below the craggy gritstone fringe of the high moorland. As the level path leads north-east there are good views of the crumbling outcrop of Great Dove Stone Rocks to the right.

Dovestone Reservoir with Great Dove Stone Rocks

B At a gate on the left by a larch plantation, a signpost indicates the option of a reservoir edge footpath.

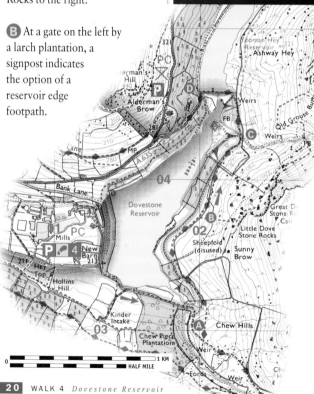

This goes down a grassy slope and is not suitable for pushchairs or wheelchairs, however. The level, surfaced route continues ahead.

C Walk 400 yds (365m) further on and immediately beyond another gate to reach several picnic tables on a grassy area on the left. This is also where the reservoir edge path rejoins the main route. The way continues ahead as a broad track and goes over the dam of the Yeoman Hey Reservoir, providing more fine views north.

D Once across the dam, turn left. After walking a further 30 yds (27m), go left again through a small metal gate with an unobtrusive sign indicating Dove Stone Car Park. The track leads down to the water's edge, this being the tricky part of the circuit for wheelchairs. It then continues, level and well-surfaced, curving below Alderman's Hill.

Soon the reservoir outflow and control tower are reached. To the left, a metal gate leads on to a bridge. The car park is now visible ahead, with the path following the crest of the grass-faced Dovestone Reservoir dam. As you complete the last stretch of the walk, have a final glimpse ahead to the sharp skyline of Wimberry Rocks. ●

Alderman's Hill and Dovestone Reservoir

5

Robin Hood's Stride and Cratcliffe Tor

From Birchover, this walk goes downhill across fields to join the Limestone Way before heading north and uphill, to investigate the outcrops of Robin Hood's Stride and Cratcliffe Tor, together with a mysterious cave. After climbing back to Birchover, the circuit ends with a look at the remarkable carved features of Rowtor Rocks.

START Birchover
DISTANCE 2½ miles (4.4km)
TIME 2½ hours
PARKING At the lower end of Main Street, Birchover, with consideration
ROUTE FEATURES Paths and tracks over farmland. Muddy in places. Many stiles and a significant amount of ascent. Optional scrambling. Dogs must be kept on a lead

 From the lower end of Main Street, by the unusually named inn, take the lane ahead.

? What is the unusual name of the inn at the start?

Pass the church and The Old Vicarage, then beyond a pond and gate, take a footpath on the left. This rises briefly to meet a track. Go left on the track as it curves past Rocking Stone Farm.

A At a very sharp curve, go through a stile by a white gate and turn right along a wall. A muddy path passes a ruined barn and descends past a clump of Scots pines to reach a track. Turn left here. Beyond a horse paddock the track goes downhill as a field path.

Cross a stream on a flat stone bridge, negotiate the B5056 via opposing stiles and come to a minor road, Dudwood Lane, at a small parking area by a red stone house.

B Turn right, following the Limestone Way along this quiet

PUBLIC TRANSPORT Buses from Matlock and Bakewell. Enquiry line tel. 0870 6082608
REFRESHMENTS Two pubs with outside tables in Birchover
PUBLIC TOILETS Birchover
ORDNANCE SURVEY MAP Outdoor Leisure 24 (The Peak District – White Peak area)

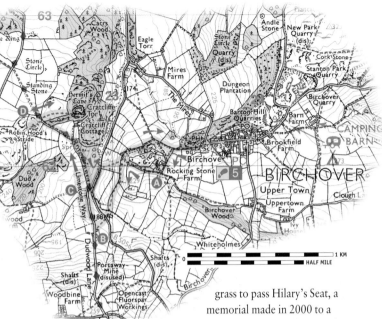

grass to pass Hilary's Seat, a memorial made in 2000 to a lady who lived in the farmstead below.

road to the bottom of a gentle slope.

C Ahead, the route continues where the Limestone Way follows a 'Private Drive'. Rise to a stone gateway, then bear half-left across

Weasel Pinnacle at Robin Hood's Stride

Robin Hood's Stride is sometimes called Mock Beggars' Hall because of its appearance as a turreted building when seen from Elton. The two pinnacles have been named 'Weasel' and 'Inaccessible' by rock climbers. Look north across two fields to see the four remaining stones of the Nine Stones Bronze Age circle.

Continue for 40 yds (37m) past a metal gate.

D Here, go over the stile on the left. A path picks its way up to the sprawling outcrop of Robin Hood's Stride. After exploring, return to the stile and turn right, down the track.

Just before the metal gate is a tall wall stile on the left. Beyond this, cross a field to another stile, which gives access to the rocks and trees of Cratcliffe Tor. After exploring the area, retrace your steps to return to the track and retrace your steps down to point **D** .

The summit of Cratcliffe Tor is an area of large grit-stone boulders bushes. Take care, as the eastern edge forms a sheer drop, though the views down onto the woods below are intriguing. At the base of the out-crop, accessed to the right of the entrance stile and hidden by two yews, is a shallow

> The Reverend Thomas Eyre, who lived nearby in the 17th century, converted **Rowtor Rocks** into a retreat by carving an amazing array of armchairs, passages, rooms and steps to enhance the natural features of the outcrop.

and gloomy 'Hermit's Cave' with a carved crucifix, now protected by a wall and railings. Note to parents of young children: the red yew berries will be tempting but are poisonous.

Turn left on the B5056 for 150 yds (137m) to a stile on the right. A muddy path leads steeply uphill to a stile at the base of the conical hill tufted with trees, passed earlier. Take the track ahead back towards Birchover. Just before the Druid Inn, take the steps on the left for a look at the fascinating carved modifications to Rowtor Rocks before re-entering the village. •

'Nine Stones' circle near Robin Hood's Stride

Gradbach and Lud's Church

START Gradbach car park
DISTANCE 3 miles (4.8km)
TIME 2½ hours
PARKING Gradbach car park (free)
ROUTE FEATURES Paths and tracks, mainly through woodland. Short stretches of minor road. Some ascent involved. Muddy in places after wet weather. One (avoidable) river crossing

6

This walk initially follows the River Dane past Gradbach Mill, before climbing into woodland to visit rocky pinnacles and then discover the amazing mossy cleft of Lud's Church. Looping back through Gradbach Wood, it then takes a higher level route above the River Dane to complete the circuit.

Turn right out of the car park along the single-track road. Where the road forks, bear right through the gateposts. This drive leads down to Gradbach Mill.

> **?** *Which three initials appear on a sign on the gatepost?*

Beyond the mill the path continues towards Forest Wood. At a track, the path rises to a hairpin with a stile on the right. Bear right here, downhill, to a footbridge.

A Beyond the footbridge, at a finger-post indicating 'Danebridge and Swythamley' go straight ahead. After walking for roughly 40 yds (37m) uphill, at another finger-post, follow 'Swythamley' for a short but steep climb of some 30 yds (27m). At a third finger-post, again marked 'Swythamley', turn right.

A steadily graded path rises through the larches, oaks and birches of Forest Wood, with many bilberries at ground level.

B The path levels out at a small clearing with two rock outcrops on the right giving a fine view of the Dane Valley. There is a narrow

PUBLIC TRANSPORT None suitable
REFRESHMENTS None
PUBLIC TOILETS None
ORDNANCE SURVEY MAP Outdoor Leisure 24 (The Peak District – White Peak area)

passage through the second out-crop, great fun for kids.

Back at the clearing, a finger-post shows the way towards Lud's Church. A narrow path cuts back, almost level, through the woods. After 200 yds (183m), immediately after a tree with a small fence round it, the entrance to Lud's Church is on the right.

The moss-hung cleft of Lud's Church

C After the first few steps up, go left and down more steps. The vertical rock walls, whenever you visit, are always gloomy and green.

Continue through Lud's Church and leave the

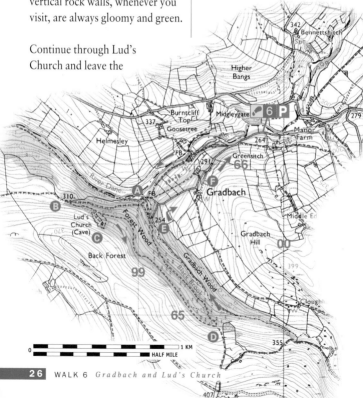

The gritstone cleft of **Lud's Church** was reputedly the religious meeting place of the Lollards in the 14th century. It has also been suggested that Lud's Church is the Green Chapel mentioned in the poem 'Sir Gawain and the Green Knight'.

top end of it via a flight of rock steps. The path contours across the wooded slope. Ignore a sign showing a way to the ridge on the right.

After a further 30 yds (27m), another post indicates 'Roach End'. Follow this line, watching for the many tree roots in the path. Among large beech trees, where the ridge seems to be dipping down, there is a further finger-post.

D Go left here, aiming for 'Gradbach'. After an initial steep descent, the path undulates through the woods. Ignore an un-official path forking off to the right.

E The path dips again and reaches the Black Brook at a multiple finger-post. Cross the river on convenient boulders. Opposite, a 'concession bridleway' takes an

obvious track, which climbs to the buildings at Gradbach.

After very wet weather the stream may be impassable. If so, simply follow the sign 'Danebridge Foot-path Only' for 100 yds (91m) to the footbridge crossed earlier on the walk. Follow the wall up to the stile and take the uphill track at the hairpin, straight ahead. Beyond a ladder-stile, the track reaches a gate marked 'Peter Watson Camping Grounds'. Go over the stile before the house, then bear right up to a surfaced road near the buildings at Gradbach.

F Whichever route you have taken, from this point just follow the tarmac track back to the car park. ●

Near Gradbach Mill

7 Tissington Trail and Village

This gentle walk makes use of a former railway line, now the Tissington Trail. Beyond a cutting, there are extensive views over the attractive White Peak landscape towards Parwich. Leaving the Trail, the route then returns across undulating fields to the estate village of Tissington with its Hall, neat stone houses, pond and five wells.

START Tissington Trail car park
DISTANCE 2½ miles (4km)
TIME 2 hours
PARKING Tissington Trail car park (pay and display)
ROUTE FEATURES Fairly level tracks and field paths. Some stiles. Can be muddy in places. Dogs must be kept on a lead

 Leave the car park along the Tissington Trail in a north-easterly direction, going under a bridge by a signpost.

> **Which three places are named on this signpost?**

The track curves left, initially in a cutting fringed with trees. Ignore a footpath crossing the trail via a flight of steps.

Once the Ashbourne to Buxton railway line, the disused track was bought by the Peak Park Planning Board and opened to walkers and cyclists in 1971.

The sides of the cutting gradually decline to reveal an undulating landscape with Shaw's Farm down to the right where the slope falls away. The trail is lined with hawthorn, blackberry and ash as it approaches another small cutting and bridge. Beyond this are further views across the valley of the Bletch Brook.

PUBLIC TRANSPORT Limited bus services to Derby and Ashbourne. Enquiry line tel. 0870 6082608
REFRESHMENTS Picnic area at Tissington Trail car park. Tearooms The Old Coach House in Tissington
PUBLIC TOILETS Tissington Trail car park
ORDNANCE SURVEY MAP Outdoor Leisure 24 (Peak District – White Peak area)

Ⓐ Walk 300 yds (274m) further on, by a finger-post to Tissington on the left take the stile and follow the path half-right to the field edge. The path continues along the edges of the fields, with two sections running between drystone walls. These can be muddy due to trampling by cattle.

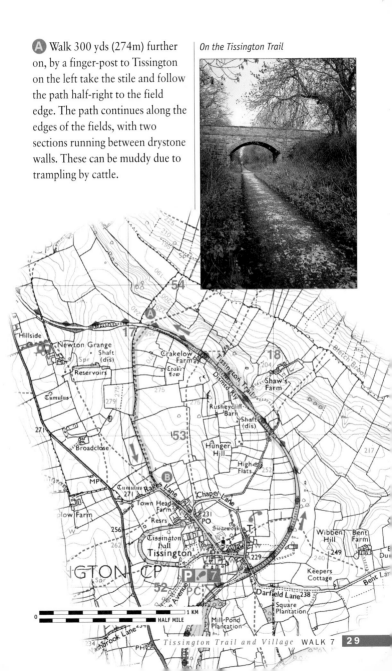

On the Tissington Trail

Tissington Hall is a Jacobean mansion built in 1609. It is still lived in by the Fitzherbert family, who have held the Tissington Estate since the reign of Elizabeth I. Opposite the Hall is Hall Well, one of five wells in Tissington which are the focus of the **Well Dressing**. This custom is a thanksgiving for the reliable water supply provided by the wells and involves the local community in the production of huge pictures, made entirely from natural materials such as clay, petals, cones and leaves.

Pass through a metal gate at the end of the second walled section. Soon, just beyond a pond on the left, there is an obvious 'ridge and furrow' pattern in the sloping field on the left.

The curved ridges in the pasture to the left are evidence of ploughing by oxen in medieval times. In order to turn at the end of each furlong, the lumbering team of oxen pulling the plough needed to begin their sweep about 20 yds (18m) before reaching the edge of the field. This has been preserved in the grassland of the field as a 'ridge and furrow' pattern.

After the final field, enter a roughly surfaced, walled lane **B**. This soon leads to a minor road, Rakes Lane, which is followed ahead, back into the village of Tissington. Continue past the hall on the right and the church on the left, to a junction. Go left here and follow the road ahead. This soon bears right to reach the starting point at the Tissington Trail car park entrance.

Tissington Hall

Wildboarclough and Shutlingsloe

8

START Clough House car park
DISTANCE 3 miles (4.8km)
TIME 2½ hours
PARKING Clough House car park (free)
ROUTE FEATURES Paths and minor roads. Several stiles. 770ft (230m) of ascent. Walk facing traffic on minor roads. Dogs must be kept on a lead

Beginning from a remote car park, this route gradually ascends to the summit of Shutlingsloe, sometimes grandiosely called the 'Cheshire Matterhorn'. There are excellent views before an initially steep descent and return via the scattered settlement of Wildboarclough with possible refreshment, a flood memorial and a couple of stately buildings.

Leave the car park by the rear entrance, over a bridge and then turn right into the yard at Clough House. The wooden gate on the left at the end of the yard is way-marked. Turn right here, across an often muddy field to a footbridge.

A Opposite, a stile gives on to a nicely graded track signposted to 'Langley via Shutlingsloe'. The way crosses a wall stile, then continues briefly alongside a pine plantation. This stretch can be muddy. The path follows a drystone wall to Banktop, then takes an access road for 100 yds (91m).

B At a gate and cattle-grid, go sharply back uphill, initially on a well-surfaced track. Climb to a gateway where yellow arrows show the way left, up a grassy slope. Via stiles, the path reaches rougher terrain. A flight of steps has been built into the slope at one point to combat footpath erosion.

C At the stile immediately above these steps, go half-right and, after

PUBLIC TRANSPORT None suitable
REFRESHMENTS Picnic tables at car park. Crag Inn (see text) welcomes children, does lunchtime food and has outside tables
PUBLIC TOILETS None
ORDNANCE SURVEY MAP Outdoor Leisure 24 (The Peak District – White Peak area)

The view east from Shutlingsloe summit

a few yards, at a finger-post, go right. The path contours past rushy patches, to a ladder-stile. Beyond this stile, go half-left into a small valley of eroded shale. At the head of this valley the path levels off and negotiates a boggy hollow via a single plank near a small wooden enclosure, before continuing to another stile.

D Do not cross this stile. Instead, go sharp left on a path of flagstones with Shutlingsloe's summit cone ahead. The path steepens, with some big steps up, before suddenly reaching the summit, which is adorned by a triangulation pillar and a circular metal topograph set in a rock. The views from here are superb. Shutlingsloe, at just 1,660ft (506m), is sometimes fancifully described as the 'Cheshire Matterhorn'.

Shutlingsloe from above Wildboarclough

Just a couple of yards from the summit pillar, the way down is shown by a yellow arrow. The path picks its way steeply down among projecting rocks and distinctly red soil. The angle soon eases as the path descends to the three-way finger-post met earlier. The outward route is now retraced as far as the cattle-grid at point **B**, just south of Banktop.

Continue down the tarmac access road to a minor road at the bottom. **E** If you are visiting the Crag Inn for refreshment, go right here for 100 yds (91m). Otherwise, turn sharp left on the minor road, then very soon go right, at the bridge over the Clough Brook.

A memorial on the Clough Brook bridge records the Wildboarclough Flood disaster, which destroyed the original structure.

On what date did this disaster occur?

Go up this quiet road, passing an impressive private house on the left. This house was once a carpet factory and more recently a post office.

F At a road junction, turn left, following the 'Macclesfield Forest' direction. Initially this single-track road passes buildings on the left before levelling off to provide excellent views across the valley to Shutlingsloe. Soon the road dips towards Clough House and the car park.

9 *Chatsworth Park and Edensor*

This enjoyable stroll begins across parkland by the River Derwent, giving fine views of the frontage of Chatsworth House, before exploring the attractive sandstone village of Edensor. It continues uphill across the deerpark with extensive views and the chance of seeing fallow deer, before crossing a wooded ridge to follow a pleasant valley back to Calton Lees.

START Calton Lees

DISTANCE 4 miles (6.4km)

TIME 3 hours

PARKING Calton Lees (free)

ROUTE FEATURES Paths and tracks through parkland and woodland. Muddy in places after wet spells. Moderate ascent involved. Dogs must be kept on a lead in the Chatsworth estate

Start this route from Calton Lees car park and take the surfaced path to a white gate and cattle-grid. Cross the road and go down to the ruined remains of the corn mill. Turn left along the bank of the broad River Derwent. Stay by the bank for views of two impressive weirs though there is open access for people to picnic and walk where they wish on this part of the estate.

The imposing sight of Chatsworth House lies across the river. Beyond a short stretch of fenced-off riverbank lies a bridge of warm sandstone. Cross this and at a cattle-grid a few yards along the road, go left across the grass for a close inspection of Queen Mary's Bower.

Ⓐ Return to the bridge and, immediately beyond it, take the

PUBLIC TRANSPORT Buses from Matlock and Bakewell. Enquiry line tel. 0870 6082608

REFRESHMENTS Kiosk and picnic area at Calton Lees car park. Tearoom at Edensor post office. Picnicking allowed on Chatsworth estate. Tearooms and pubs with gardens/outside tables serving lunchtime food in Baslow, 3 miles (4.8km) north

PUBLIC TOILETS At garden centre close to Calton Lees car park. Also at Edensor tearoom

ORDNANCE SURVEY MAP Outdoor Leisure 24 (The Peak District – White Peak area)

obvious path leading ahead and gently uphill. As this rounds a low ridge among scattered trees, the spire of Edensor church comes into sight. The path dips to a road, with the entrance to Edensor directly opposite. The post office lies to the left and the church fills the view ahead.

? *What kind of barrier is there in the road at the entrance to Edensor village?*

Follow the main village road to the right of the church and then look out for a finger-post announcing

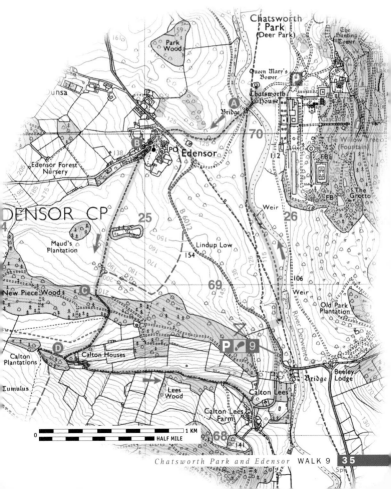

'Footpath to Rowsley 3m', just before a grassy slope on the left.

B Multiple short flights of steps lead to a gate atop a stile with open parkland beyond. A low wooden post 40 yds (37m) away, half-right, shows the line to take. Continue in the same direction, passing a discreet yellow arrow on a post by a tree. Keep an eye open for fallow deer in this area.

The current **Chatsworth House** was created by the first Duke of Devonshire between 1686 and 1707. The Hunting Tower on the high ground behind the mansion is older, dating from the 1550s. Queen Mary's Bower was a summer retreat said to have been used by Mary Queen of Scots several times in the 1570s. The fourth Duke engaged **Lancelot 'Capability' Brown** in 1760 to redesign the grounds. This involved the building of the now ruined corn mill. In 1843 the sixth Duke had the 290-ft (90-m) Emperor Fountain added to the gardens.

The path passes the right-hand end of a plantation bounded by a wooden fence then rises, still on the same course. Continue uphill, passing to the right-hand side of a further small copse and an isolated waymark, to reach a tall wall at the edge of the deer park.

Return to the bridge and, immediately beyond it, take the

Looking south along the River Derwent

The front view of Chatsworth House

obvious path leading ahead and gently uphill. As this rounds a low ridge among scattered trees, the spire of Edensor church comes into sight. The path dips to a road, with the entrance to Edensor directly opposite. The post office lies to the left and the church fills the view ahead.

C Go through the gate to avoid climbing the huge stile and follow the wide track uphill through woodland. Just beyond the crest of the rise, at a gate where the woodland ends, the view suddenly opens out. Follow the path as it goes forward across a pasture then veers slightly right to reach a gritstone wall. Here the path turns right, parallel to the wall, as it drops towards Calton Houses.

D Beyond a gate the bridleway curves as a badly gullied track down to the hamlet, before zig-zagging into the valley bottom. It then descends steadily for more than 1/2 mile (800m) until, by the attractive cluster of stone buildings at Calton Lees Farm, it meets a tarmac surface. This is taken as it swings left and levels out to return to the Calton Lees car park ●

10 Monk's Dale and the Limestone Way

Beginning from a converted station at Miller's Dale, this walk initially follows the Monsal Trail along the old railway track. It descends steeply to cross the River Wye, then climbs via the Limestone Way, with excellent views, to the high plateau. The return leg threads through the meadows, outcrops and ancient woodland of the Monk's Dale nature reserve.

START Miller's Dale
DISTANCE $3\frac{1}{2}$ miles (5.6km)
TIME 3 hours
PARKING Miller's Dale station car park (pay and display)
ROUTE FEATURES Paths and tracks through farmland and woodland. Can be very muddy after wet spells. Limestone underfoot is notoriously slippery when wet. Save this walk for a dry day. Moderate ascent involved

From the old station platform at Miller's Dale take the Monsal Trail left. This leads over one of two huge parallel bridges. After 400 yds (365m) a finger-post points left. Descend a steep path, where the limestone underfoot is slippery after rain, to reach a footbridge over the River Wye.

A Go left for a few yards to the remains of the Miller's Dale Meal Mill, where there is an information

In the 1860s the Midland Railway line between Buxton and Matlock was built through **Miller's Dale**, where a quiet hamlet is wedged into the steep-sided valley of the Wye. The line was closed in 1968 but reopened in 1981 as the Monsal Trail, a recreational route for walkers and cyclists.

board alongside the 13ft (4m) diameter wheel. Take the few steps opposite the wheel and turn right on the B6049.

PUBLIC TRANSPORT Buses from Buxton, Sheffield, Chesterfield, Mansfield and Derby. Enquiry line tel. 0870 6082608
REFRESHMENTS Friendly café opposite car park entrance. Pub in Miller's Dale with outside tables and lunchtime food
PUBLIC TOILETS Miller's Dale station car park
CHILDREN'S PLAY AREA Opposite car park
ORDNANCE SURVEY MAP Outdoor Leisure 24 (The Peak District – White Peak area)

After another 30 yds (27m), bear left up a steep, narrow road announced as 'Unsuitable for Motors'. You are now on the Limestone Way, a walking route that links the towns of Matlock and Castleton.

B Very soon, follow a Limestone Way fingerpost on the left. The path cuts back, still climbing steeply. There are impressive views across Monk's Dale to the station where the walk began and the flat-topped summit of Knot Low. To the south across Miller's Dale are towering grey slopes which once rang to the sound of limestone quarrying.

Knot Low from Monksdale Farm

Beyond a gate, go through the yard of Monksdale Farm and leave it on the left, enjoying more splendid views. Continue gaining height on a track between drystone walls. This skirts a side valley then strikes across the plateau, providing wide views of the fields parcelled by limestone walls.

The track continues ahead for ¹/₂ mile (800m), initially gaining height then gently dipping. The latter part of this green lane across the plateau can be very muddy after prolonged rain.

C At Monksdale House Farm, go left on a minor road, dropping into an obvious valley. At the bottom of the dip, leave the Limestone Way to go through a squeeze stile on the left. Follow the stream and enter the National Nature Reserve of Monk's Dale.

Cross a grassy meadow and take the path between narrowing

Monk's Dale takes its name from **Monksdale Farm**, which is built on the site of a grange and chapel established here by Lenton Abbey near Nottingham.

limestone walls with a stream alongside. Here, enter moss-festooned woodland which has an aura of great age. The path is very rocky as it twists along the floor of the valley, and again the limestone can be treacherous in wet conditions.

D After a while the path climbs out on the left across a broad slope patterned with boulders and some hawthorn bushes. The path rises across this slope, giving fine views across the landscape, before dropping again to come close to the stream.

At a footbridge the path switches to the right bank of the stream. Climbing a few easy rock steps, it mounts a final mound and drops to a gate. Do not go through this gate. Instead take a rising grassy path on the right. Farm buildings are soon reached beyond a gate at the boundary of the nature reserve.

An adjacent stile leads out to a minor road. Follow this briefly downhill to see on your left, a friendly café and on your right, the Miller's Dale station car park. ●

> **?** *What is the name of the café near Miller's Dale station?*

A drystone wall on the Limestone Way near Monksdale House

11 *Langsett Reservoir*

This walk begins in woods by the shore of Langsett Reservoir before climbing on to the heather moors of Hingcliff Common, where there are fine open views and the strong chance of an encounter with red grouse. Beyond more woodland, the route visits the attractive hamlet of Upper Midhope before returning to Langsett across the reservoir dam.

START Langsett Barn
DISTANCE 3½ miles (5.6km)
TIME 2½ hours
PARKING Langsett Barn (free)
ROUTE FEATURES Mainly moorland and woodland paths and tracks. One short stretch of road. Moderate ascent involved. Dogs must be on a lead. Moors may be closed on a few days each autumn for grouse-shooting

Near the picnic tables by the car park, a finger-post indicates a 'Circular Walk' and points to a gate.

> **?** *Which two initials appear on this signpost?*

Almost immediately after this, branch left down into the woods. The path, which descends over a bed of pine needles to a wall above the reservoir shoreline, is fairly level, but keep an eye open for stones, mud and particularly tree roots.

Just before the woods end, the path angles uphill. Leaving the mature woodland, it passes through an area of young ash, oak and birch planted in 1994. The sturdy stone structure of Brookhouse Bridge is soon visible on the left and the path dips to reach it.

Ⓐ At the gate on the bridge the 'Boundary of Open Country' is reached. Here the moors begin.

PUBLIC TRANSPORT Buses from Barnsley, Penistone and Holmfirth. SYPTE Traveline tel. 01709 515151
REFRESHMENTS Picnic area at Langsett Barn car park. Pub with tables and lunchtime food at Langsett. Also small café nearby
PUBLIC TOILETS At Langsett Barn
ORDNANCE SURVEY MAP Outdoor Leisure 1 (The Peak District – Dark Peak area)

A track twists to the left and winds steeply up alongside the edge of a plantation before striking ahead for the open moorland. Among the heather and bilberry and broken gritstone walls, red grouse are almost certain to be seen and heard.

A wooden post, again labelled 'YW Circular Walk', stands at the highest point of the circuit, 1073ft (327m) above

The distinctive call of the **red grouse** is likely to be heard before the birds are seen, though their low curving flight is one of the most evocative sights of the moors. The patchwork of heather seen on this walk shows how moorland management works. The long patches provide cover for nesting and shelter, while the newly burnt areas give the grouse their favourite food – young heather shoots.

sea-level. Here an obvious path leads off left, slightly downhill at first and then gently uphill to the ruins of North America Farm.

B Continue through a gate beyond the tumbled ruins, following the track as it dips to come alongside the larch and pine plantation of Mauk Royd. Descending steadily, the track crosses the Thickwoods Brook and rises to a metal gate.

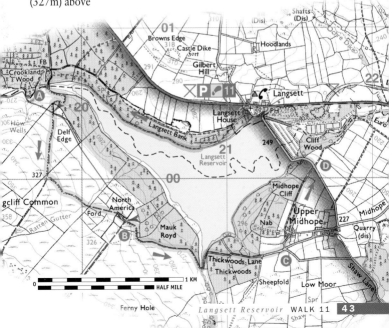

From here it continues as Thickwoods Lane, a roughly surfaced track on a broad ride between trees, to a further gate. Beyond the gate is a short, concrete 'Privilege Footpath' leading to a sharp bend on a minor road.

> **North America Farm** was abandoned when the Langsett Reservoir was constructed, to safeguard against the pollution of streams feeding the reservoir. It was used for target practice prior to the **Normandy Landings** in 1944, while Thickwoods Lane was used for tank access, hence the brick surface.

Reservoir. Take the footpath by the road across the dam, passing below the valve house, the highly distinctive design of which is based on the remarkable gatehouse of Lancaster Castle.

C Ignore the road itself, and turn left up a steep grassy lane by a 'YW Circular Walk' sign. This climbs to the quiet stone hamlet of Upper Midhope. Turn left at Upper Midhope to find a footpath finger-post by a wooden post. Go right, as indicated, alongside a wall, to meet a metalled track which eases down to a minor road.

D A left turn here leads downhill, round a curve and down to the dam which holds back Langsett

> Construction work began on **Langsett Reservoir** in 1889 and continued for 15 years. A huge community of navvies lived in a corrugated iron 'Tin Town', equipped with a canteen, a doctor's house, an isolation hospital and recreation facilities. Today, the reservoir supplies northern Sheffield with 60,000 cubic metres of water per day.

The minor road you are on reaches the A616 at the small settlement of Langsett. Go left and immediately beyond the Wagon and Horses, turn into the large pub yard and follow your nose, taking a short, surfaced road between a cluster of attractive houses. This leads back to the Langsett Barn car park. ●

Thickwoods Brook

Youlgreave and the River Lathkill

12

START Youlgreave
DISTANCE 4½ miles (7.2km)
TIME 3½ hours
PARKING In Youlgreave village, with consideration
ROUTE FEATURES Riverside and farmland paths. Moderate ascent involved. Some stiles

Beginning from the White Peak village of Youlgreave, this walk descends to the bank of the River Bradford. Passing water meadows and crags en route to Alport, it then follows the equally beautiful River Lathkill before climbing over the limestone plateau to return to Youlgreave.

From the centre of Youlgreave take Holywell Lane, which tilts down past the Wesleyan chapel and village hall to the River Bradford. Turn sharp left and follow the riverbank, watching for trout in the clear water.

Both the **River Bradford**, which is barely 2 miles (3.2km) long, and the **Lathkill** are renowned trout streams. Charles Cotton said the Lathkill was 'by many degrees, the purest and most transparent stream that I ever yet saw, either at home or abroad.'

A Cross a minor road and continue through a gate labelled 'No Cars'. The track switches to the south bank of the stream. Do not cross the small arched bridge on the left, but follow the track ahead below the vertical crag of Rhienstor.

A further gate announces that an important population of water voles lives in this area. In summer swathes of flowers, including meadow cranesbill, scabious and drifts of meadowsweet, colour this area. Almost level walking leads to the minor road at Alport.

B Cross over by the phone box and take the footpath signposted to

PUBLIC TRANSPORT Buses from Bakewell and Sheffield. Enquiry line tel. 0870 6082608
REFRESHMENTS Several pubs and a café in Youlgreave
PUBLIC TOILETS In Youlgreave
ORDNANCE SURVEY MAP Outdoor Leisure 24 (The Peak District – White Peak area)

'Conksbury'. A series of stiles marks the way ahead with the River Lathkill close by, on the right, but not always visible.

? *What colour is the phone box?*

C Immediately beyond Raper Lodge, which is clearly seen on the left, take a brief diversion to the right on the bridleway heading for Haddon Hall. Just go as far as the bridge where a semi-circular weir holds back a superb pool. The trout here are huge and will take any bread thrown into the water in spectacular fashion.

Return to the footpath and, turning right, continue to a minor road. Go right again and walk facing the possible traffic for the few awkward yards downhill to Conksbury Bridge.

The River Lathkill flows over **Carboniferous limestone**, a pervious rock with weaknesses, called joints and bedding planes, which are very gradually eroded by the effect of water. When these are widened sufficiently, the entire volume of the river can run underground in the rock. This is the case at **Lathkill Lodge**, where the river disappears after long dry spells.

reaching the white house at Lathkill Lodge.

E It comes as a shock to discover that, except in the wettest of times, the boulder-strewn riverbed here is dry. A footbridge provides the easiest way to cross in all conditions. From the bridge take the track rising at a steady gradient, with a single hairpin, to reach a gate.

D The footpath now takes the north bank of the Lathkill. This is a popular picnicking area, with grassy flats by a series of delightful weirs and pools. High on the open valley side the buildings at the edge of Over Haddon are visible.

Beyond the weirs the path negotiates a small rock step, then narrows among vegetation before

River Lathkill near Conksbury Bridge

The path is indicated, going half-right across the fields of the high plateau to Meadow Place Grange. The way is clearly marked, via stiles, as it passes among the extensive farm buildings. Rising further, with wide views back over Lathkill Dale to Over Haddon, the field path reaches a minor road.

F Go briefly right on this road before taking a path on the left. This passes through a couple of squeeze stiles and crosses the head of a shallow valley to reach a rough track. Youlgreave is now seen across fields half-left. Continue ahead until the track reaches a minor road, then turn left to enter Youlgreave on Moor Lane. ●

13 *Thor's Cave and Beeston Tor*

From Wetton this walk crosses the limestone plateau to Thor's Cave before descending steeply to follow the line of an old railway alongside the River Manifold. Negotiating the river by stepping stones near the dramatic face of Beeston Tor, the route then climbs back to the plateau, providing wide views on the return leg to Wetton.

START Wetton
DISTANCE 3½ miles (5.6km)
TIME 3 hours
PARKING Wetton car park (free)
ROUTE FEATURES Farmland and riverside paths and tracks. Stepping stones (optional). Stiles and many steps. Considerable ascent involved. Dogs must be kept on a lead

From the stile at the village end of the car park, walk along a gently rising track. Just beyond a farmyard, turn left along the road. After walking for some 100 yds (91m), bear half-right at a road junction.

Ⓐ Walk on for another 30 yds (27m), by a track on the left, a finger-post indicates a concession path between drystone walls to Thor's Cave. The spire of Grindon church is prominent beyond the wooded cleft of the Manifold Valley.

Pass a wooden gate and 50 yds (46m) further on a finger-post and notice on the right indicate 'Thor's Cave over stile'. Cross the stile and go left by the wall, soon contouring across the head of a steep valley. This area is often muddy. Beyond another stile, the path is surfaced with limestone chippings as it leads to Thor's Cave.

From just below the cave mouth, a long flight of steps leads steeply down, then levels off before tilting again, down to a footbridge over the River Manifold.

PUBLIC TRANSPORT None suitable
REFRESHMENTS Pub in Wetton with family room and outside tables
PUBLIC TOILETS At Wetton car park
ORDNANCE SURVEY MAP Outdoor Leisure 24 (The Peak District – White Peak area)

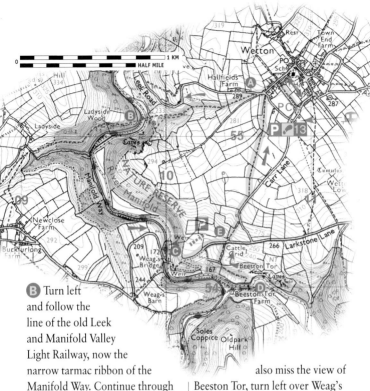

B Turn left and follow the line of the old Leek and Manifold Valley Light Railway, now the narrow tarmac ribbon of the Manifold Way. Continue through the car park before Weag's Bridge.

C If you wish to avoid the stepping stones, though you will

Thor's Cave, thought to be named for the Norse God of Thunder, has a floor of angled bedrock and clay which needs care, particularly when it's wet. Partial excavation in the 19th century revealed flint arrow-heads, bronze brooches and a complete skeleton, thought to be **Neolithic**, buried in an upright position. From the cave mouth there is a fine view north along the Manifold Valley.

also miss the view of Beeston Tor, turn left over Weag's Bridge and follow the minor road as it zigzags up past two hairpins as far as a cattle-grid.

For the main route, take the right-hand of the two lanes by the river beyond Weag's Bridge. Soon the towering crag of Beeston Tor comes into view ahead. 100 yds (91m) before a derelict wooden shed, cross a stile on the left, onto the adjacent farm access road. Continue over a wide bridge at the confluence of the Hamps and Manifold rivers.

Beeston Tor

E This is where the alternative route, avoiding the stepping stones, rejoins the main route description. A few yards beyond the cattle-grid, on the left between two gateways, take an unmarked stile.

The path rises steeply across a field to meet another minor road, Carr Lane, which is followed for 200 yds (183m) to a stile on the left. From here the buildings of Wetton can be made out, half-right. To the north and west, there are fine, open views across the plateau.

D After 50 yds (46m) a leaning finger-post points through an old wooden gate on the left. The river-bed is usually dry here, though there are stepping-stones. In very exceptional circumstances even these may be under water, in which case retreat to Weag's Bridge.

There are fine views of the face of Beeston Tor from here. Cross the river then, 20 yds (18m) left of the stepping stones, take the stile and go ahead to a left-pointing finger-post. Follow a well-graded path up a grassy shelf to a gate and squeeze-stile. Bear right here, following a wall to the minor road which has come from Weag's Bridge. Turn right on the road.

Head across several fields, aiming just left of Wetton church tower to locate the stiles. This stretch can be muddy, especially round the stiles.

At the edge of Wetton pass left of the farm buildings and look for two stiles which allow passage along the edge of a garden, to a road junction. From here retrace the route back to the car park. ●

Crowden and Torside Reservoir

From Crowden, this walk climbs briefly to join the Pennine Way. It then drops to the Torside Reservoir dam to reach the Longdendale Trail. This provides easy, level walking for nearly 2 miles (3.2km), before a more varied low-level path is taken round the eastern end of Torside Reservoir back to Crowden. Throughout, the views of the surrounding gritstone landscape are superb.

START Crowden. Note: Torside is an alternative starting point, in which case the route description should be read starting at point **D**

DISTANCE 4 miles (6.4km)

TIME 3 hours

PARKING Crowden car park or Torside car park (both free)

ROUTE FEATURES Paths and tracks, mostly fairly straightforward. Steep steps in a couple of places. Dogs must be kept on a lead

From the Crowden car park, follow the sign to the toilets and turn right on a walled lane in front of these. At a finger-post indicating

Crowden was once a busy hamlet with a Tudor-style hall built in 1692 for the Hatfield family. The hall fell into disrepair and was demolished by Manchester Corporation in 1937. Its former location is now occupied by the campsite. A terrace of cottages nearby, called Stone Row, has been converted into a youth hostel.

the Pennine Way, go left between the campsite and a wooden barn. The track crosses the Crowden Brook and rises to join the Pennine Way just before it reaches the upper edge of a plantation.

A Continue ahead on the roughly surfaced track which rises slightly more before dipping downhill to the A628. Cross this busy trans-Pennine road with care. Immediately opposite, the Pennine Way continues as a path, going down a

PUBLIC TRANSPORT National Express coaches between Manchester and Sheffield stop at Crowden. Tel. 08705 808080. Limited bus services from Huddersfield, Holmfirth, Glossop and Sheffield to Torside. Tel. 0870 608 2608

REFRESHMENTS Picnic tables at Crowden car park

PUBLIC TOILETS Crowden car park and Torside car park

ORDNANCE SURVEY MAP Outdoor Leisure 1 (The Peak District – Dark Peak area)

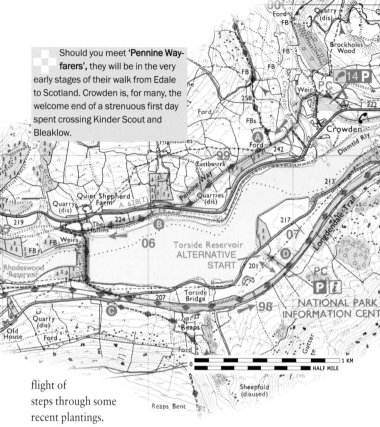

Should you meet **'Pennine Way-farers',** they will be in the very early stages of their walk from Edale to Scotland. Crowden is, for many, the welcome end of a strenuous first day spent crossing Kinder Scout and Bleaklow.

Torside Reservoir
ALTERNATIVE
START

flight of
steps through some
recent plantings.

B The path soon enters a narrow belt of mature pines and follows this westwards, with Torside Reservoir now close by on the left. The way eventually leads down, across a water conduit, to the massive dam.

> **?** *Check the map to find the name of the reservoir lying way below on your right.*

This is an impressive viewpoint, with the waters of Torside Reservoir stretching away to the left. Ahead lie the brooding slopes of Peaknaze Moor. Go left at the end of the dam, up the access road to a small paved area by the B6105, passing under the prominent electricity lines which disfigure the valley.

C At this point our route leaves the Pennine Way as we go left,

E Where the trail comes alongside the road, a finger-post points left for Crowden and a path cuts back briefly at 180° to reach the road at a gate. Directly opposite the Torside concessionary path follows a broad track which winds down through larch woodland to a long, curving footbridge.

At the end of the bridge, take the very steep steps down on the left and follow a well-made path alongside a water channel. After some distance, ignore the stone bridge parapets on the right. When you reach a gate, turn right to the main road. Turn right again on the footway by the road for 50 yds (46m) or so, then cross carefully and return to the car park at the starting point. ●

The Longdendale Trail

> The **Longdendale Trail** forms part of the longer **Trans-Pennine Trail**, which links Liverpool and Hull. It occupies the line of the first rail link, the Woodhead Pass, between Sheffield and Manchester, which was opened in 1845. Long closed to rail traffic, the route has now been modified for the use of walkers and cyclists.

along the level, well-surfaced Longdendale Trail. After 1/2 mile (800m) the view opens out to the right, with Torside Clough showing as a huge scoop in the flank of Bleaklow.

D In a further 500 yds (457m), at a gated stone enclosure, there is a choice of two paths on the left. These allow a brief diversion to the Torside car park, where public toilets are available all year. As mentioned above, this is also an alternative starting point for the circuit. Whether you start from here or not, continue along the Longdendale Trail for another mile (1.6km) or so.

15 *Monuments on the Eastern Moors*

This walk encompasses several superb viewpoints, following Birchen Edge to Nelson's Monument and the Three Ships, before crossing damp ground to reach an ancient route across Eaglestone Flat. It then visits Wellington's Monument and the Eagle Stone before dropping through woodland to a packhorse bridge, from where an attractive return across rough ground completes the circuit.

START Birchen Edge car park
DISTANCE 4 miles (6.4km)
TIME 3 hours
PARKING Birchen Edge car park (free), off the A619 adjacent to the Robin Hood pub. Note: please do not park in pub car park unless you are a customer
ROUTE FEATURES Paths on heather moors and rough grazing land are wet in places. Some boulders. Some stiles. Moderate ascent involved. Dogs must be kept on a lead

Turn left out of the car park and walk up by the minor road for 50 yds (46m) to a stile providing entry to the Access Land of the Eastern Moors Estate. Go ahead on a sandy path leading through birches and bracken.

By a large boulder on the left, you have the choice of continuing ahead below the crags of Birchen Edge, which will allow views of the activities of rock climbers, or turning right to follow the crest of the moorland and the rocky edge. The paths rejoin later.

A The latter choice, turning right, is recommended. From the boulder a steep, rocky path rises to the moorland where it turns left to head north, gaining height as it weaves among the heather and gritstone boulders and sheep.

PUBLIC TRANSPORT Buses from Bakewell, Chesterfield and Matlock. Enquiry line tel. 0870 6082608
REFRESHMENTS Robin Hood pub, adjacent to start, provides lunchtime meals and has a beer garden. Pubs and tearooms in Baslow, 1½ miles (2.4km) west
PUBLIC TOILETS In Baslow
ORDNANCE SURVEY MAP Outdoor Leisure 24 (The Peak District – White Peak area)

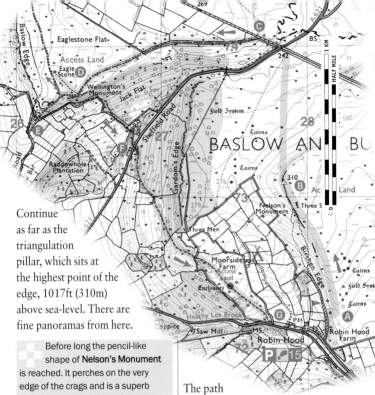

Continue as far as the triangulation pillar, which sits at the highest point of the edge, 1017ft (310m) above sea-level. There are fine panoramas from here.

Before long the pencil-like shape of **Nelson's Monument** is reached. It perches on the very edge of the crags and is a superb viewpoint, with the **Three Ships** just a few yards away. These carvings honour the successes of Nelson at the battles of the Nile in 1798 and Trafalgar in 1805.

? *What are the Three Ships called?*

B Immediately north of the pillar, go down a heathery gully, from where a narrow path soon meets a broader path going due north. Despite a few short stretches of duck-board, this area is often very wet.

The path leads very gradually downhill to a stile at a crossroads. Turn left and take the minor road opposite, marked with a 3T sign, for 150 yds (137m), to a gate on the left.

C Easy walking now follows on the broad, almost level track stretching ahead. There are scattered birches to the left, and upland fields and rough moorland to the right. The track passes an ancient stone guidepost, carved 'Chesterfeild Roade', before reaching Wellington's Monument on a prominent rock outcrop. This is another dramatic viewpoint.

Continue, with the track rising gently, for a further 100 yds (91m). **D** At this point, an optional diversion can be made, out and back, to the massive Eagle Stone which can be seen squatting on the moor a little to the north.

The Eagle Stone, 25ft (8m) high, is an isolated block of gritstone which, long ago, was traditionally climbed by the young men of Baslow to prove their manhood.

The track now begins to dip south-west past a series of disused quarries at the southern end of Baslow Edge on the right, before curving round to a gate.

E Do not go through the gate. Instead, bear sharp left along the

Birchen Edge, with Nelson's Monument and the Three Ships

wall on a muddy path, which is not signposted. There is a steep bracken-covered slope to your left. The path enters an oakwood dotted with mossy boulders.

Soon the path veers right and drops more steadily among birches, with a wall again on the right, to reach a substantial stile. A narrow passage beyond this leads to a packhorse bridge with a wild garden on the left.

Half-right beyond the bridge, the path reaches the busy A621, which can be crossed carefully between opposing stiles.

F The path climbs behind Cupola Cottage and continues to gain height steadily through a matrix of bracken, birches and boulders below Gardom's Edge. It levels out at a narrow gritstone gateway, with trees on a slope below, to the right.

The path heads south-east across this area of Access Land, gradually losing height. Traffic noise increases as the path dips to a stile in the field corner. **G** From here simply turn left, and take the pavement by the road, passing the Eric Byne Memorial Campsite, to the Robin Hood and completion of the route. ●

Ladybower Reservoir and Cutthroat Bridge

16

From the shore of Ladybower Reservoir this walk rises through the Ashopton Woodlands, then climbs more steeply to Lead Hill, a stunning viewpoint above the Ladybower Reservoir. A gentle descent across heather moorland leads to Cutthroat Bridge, from where an ancient route is followed, past the Ladybower Inn, giving a superb final view south towards Win Hill.

START A57, immediately east of Ashopton Viaduct
DISTANCE 4 miles (6.4km)
TIME 3 hours
PARKING Linear car park along A57 just east of Ashopton Viaduct (free)
ROUTE FEATURES Paths and tracks on gritstone and heather moorland. Considerable ascent. Dogs must be kept on a lead

From the parking area, walk towards the Ashopton Viaduct. Just before the A57 launches out across the reservoir, take a wide tarmac drive uphill on the right. This almost immediately swings sharply right again to the few buildings at Ashopton.

When the tarmac ends, a rough track continues to a grassy area surrounded by fences and walls.

Ladybower Reservoir was the last of the three dams of the Upper Derwent Valley to be built. It was completed in 1945, by which time the rising water had already swallowed the two villages of Derwent and Ashopton. Most of the evacuated villagers were rehoused at a newly built estate at Yorkshire Bridge, just south of the Ladybower Dam.

A Go through the gate on the left with a Severn Trent Water notice,

PUBLIC TRANSPORT Buses from Sheffield and Manchester. Enquiry line tel. 0870 6082608
REFRESHMENTS Ladybower Inn. Picnic tables at Heatherdene, 1 mile (1.6km) south on the A6013
PUBLIC TOILETS At Heatherdene
ORDNANCE SURVEY MAP Outdoor Leisure 1 (The Peak District – Dark Peak area)

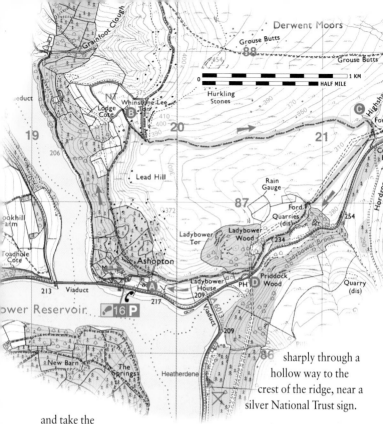

sharply through a hollow way to the crest of the ridge, near a silver National Trust sign.

and take the broad track which cuts back uphill among larches. This soon veers north and is very muddy at times. Its undulating course soon emerges from the woods and provides wide views north along the Upper Derwent Valley and west to the twin tops of Crook Hill.

The path rises alongside a drystone wall, before breaking more steeply to the right. Bad erosional gullying is a feature of the path as it rises

? *What name is on the National Trust sign?*

B At the top of the climb, take a few steps right, onto an unnamed but obvious point, and soak up the fabulous views. Win Hill rises from the opposite shore of Ladybower Reservoir, and Lose Hill and Kinder Scout can be seen further west. To the east, wild moors slope away towards Sheffield's western fringes.

Several paths meet at the point you have reached. The one you now want is the bridleway which leads east, steadily downhill. This is more or less straight ahead from the path you arrived on.

The path eventually passes to the right of a fenced area, then curves quite sharply to the right as it reaches Highshaw Clough.

Ⓒ Just before you pass under the high tension wires, bear right on a track which soon takes a direct line south-west. Below, on the left, Cutthroat Bridge is visible, carrying the busy A57. As the path crosses the moor, the cone of Win Hill is visible straight ahead. Cutthroat Bridge acquired its blood-thirsty name in 1635 when, rather myster-iously, 'a man with a wound in his throat

was found in Eashaw (Highshaw) Clough'.

After 500 yds (457m) the track drops to a metal gate where a stream is easily forded on boulders. Parts of the bridleway are muddy beyond this. There is a fairly steep descent as the track comes closer to Ladybower Wood.

The view north from Ashopton Woods, Upper Derwent

Ladybower Reservoir from Whinstone Lee Fields

D Continue down the track and head for Ladybower Inn. If you prefer to complete the route in one go, take a path on the right, which leads off at the point where the road and the pub car park become visible ahead. This is only about 40 yds (37m) before you reach the pub.

The path passes through oak woodland behind the pub before rising between a drystone wall on the left and a steep bracken-clad slope on the right.

At the crest of the rise, the wall dips away and there are sudden excellent views over the reservoir to the sharp profile of Bamford Edge and the wooded flanks of Win Hill. The path then soon dips to the grassy enclosure at point **A**, referred to earlier. From there, retrace the first part of the walk back to the car park. ●

Hayfield and Lantern Pike

17

START Hayfield
DISTANCE 5½ miles (8.9km)
TIME 4 hours
PARKING Hayfield station/Sett Valley Trail (pay and display)
ROUTE FEATURES Paths and tracks on moorland and grassy slopes. Considerable ascent involved. Many stiles. Muddy in places after wet spells. Dogs must be kept on a lead

This exploration begins by passing through the attractive stone village of Hayfield, huddled among high hills. It then takes the Snake Path, an ancient route on to the heather moors, before going through the grounds of Park Hall. A climb to the superb viewpoint of Lantern Pike is the highlight, before a return to Hayfield via the Sett Valley Trail.

Start at the car park at the former Hayfield station. Opposite the car park entrance, take the subway under the A624. Going either way out of the subway you will reach the main village street of Hayfield near The George pub. Go left for a few yards and cross the substantial stone bridge over the River Sett.

Ahead, go right into Bank Street, then continue right as it merges with Kinder Road, which is lined with the typical terraced houses of this former textile village. After about 300 yds (274m), opposite a tall iron post on the right, the Snake Path begins on the left. A famous right of way, dedicated in 1897, this is initially a track which goes uphill through several kissing-gates and passes a prominent clump of trees.

As the ground levels off the path reaches the National Trust's High Peak estate at another gate. The

PUBLIC TRANSPORT Buses to Stockport and Glossop. Enquiry line tel. 0870 6082608
REFRESHMENTS Kiosk and picnic area at Hayfield station. Cafés and pubs in Hayfield
PUBLIC TOILETS Hayfield station
ORDNANCE SURVEY MAP Outdoor Leisure 24 (The Peak District – Dark Peak area)

Snake Path, looking east

plateau of Kinder Scout fills the sky-line in the open view that lies ahead.

A At a gate 30 yds (27m) on, the route changes direction where a small post with a yellow arrow indicates a left turn. A narrow path weaves through heather on the fringe of Middle Moor, then angles downhill through bracken and rhododendrons to a wall surrounding the grounds of Park Hall.

A large gate gives access to Park Hall Woods. Swing left on a wide track among mature trees, going gently downhill, to reach Little Hayfield.

B Carefully cross the busy A624 and continue down to an old mill,

? *What is the name of the lane leading to the mill?*

which is now converted for residential purposes.

Immediately beyond the mill, turn right across two bridges and briefly take a path by the stream. This leads to a stone causey rising up a grassy slope. The path then climbs more sharply to reach an ivy-covered house. Here two stiles give on to an easier climb along a sunken track by a dry-stone wall.

There are fine views back across the valley. As higher ground is reached the gradient steadily eases, with the path finally coming to an unusual finger-post marking a six-way footpath junction.

C The path now cuts back south across the rough pasture, aiming for Lantern Pike. In reality, it is possible to harmlessly cut this corner. Once the footpath reaches the edge of the National Trust's landholding, it climbs quite steeply up to the viewfinder on the summit.

From the summit, follow the path south to a drystone wall, where it

Lantern Pike reputedly gets its name from the fact that a ruin on the summit, long since demolished, was used as a site for lighting warning beacons. The summit area of the hill was bought and donated to the **National Trust** in 1950 in memory of Edwin Royce and his 'labour in the cause of securing the freedom of the hills'. There's a superb view, informed by a topograph, particularly to the south-east over Hayfield, with the high peat plateau of Kinder Scout beyond.

Hayfield from Lantern Pike

goes left with the wall, tilting sharply down to a track. Turn right through an obvious gate and continue down to meet a minor road.

D At the road, go right then immediately left on a downhill track by a sign to Hegginbottom Farm. Follow the track round when it twists sharp left at a hairpin. After 50 yds (46m) before the farm buildings, take the footpath over a wall-stile on the right. Beyond two narrow squeeze-stiles, it drops, with one steep, sometimes muddy, section, to a hefty bridge over the River Sett.

E The path negotiates the western end of a reservoir containing a distinctive round island, before rising through a gate to meet the former railway now known as the Sett Valley Trail. Turn left here and wind down with just over 1/2 mile (800m) of level walking back to the starting point of the walk at the car park on the edge of Hayfield. ●

The Goyt Valley and Windgather Rocks

This walk features a woodland path, a long climb to Taxal Edge and Windgather Rocks, a gritstone outcrop facing west. The path continues south across high heather moors towards Pym Chair before descending alongside a Roman road called The Street to return to the valley.

START The Street car park at Errwood Reservoir. The circuit can be started from Pym Chair car park **F**. NB The road from The Street to Derbyshire Bridge is closed to traffic May–Sept Sun and Bank Hol. Mon

DISTANCE 5½ miles (8.9km)

TIME 4 hours

PARKING The Street car park or Pym Chair car park (both free)

ROUTE FEATURES There is a considerable ascent and the route may be muddy in places. Dogs must be kept on a lead

18

At the T-junction outside the car park, take the minor road towards Buxton. After just a few yards, take a path by a finger-post on the left. Beyond a gate, bear half-right, downhill, as shown by a lichen-encrusted wooden post. The grass bank of Errwood Dam is on the right.

Pass through another gate to enter open woodland high above Fernilee Reservoir. A narrow path tilts down to meet a broader track by the reservoir's shore. Continue north on this generally well-surfaced track. Watch for some muddy patches and tree roots.

At a red marker the path leaves the reservoir edge and climbs a winding flight of gentle steps to a signpost by a drystone wall. Turn right here, towards Fernilee, as the path continues north through woodland.

A The woodland ends at a gate. Go right, on a tarmac track, down to the Fernilee dam, where there are impressive views south, over the surface of the reservoir.

PUBLIC TRANSPORT None suitable

REFRESHMENTS Picnic tables at The Street car park

PUBLIC TOILETS At Bunsal Cob car park, ½ mile (800m) east of The Street

ORDNANCE SURVEY MAP Outdoor Leisure 24 (The Peak District – White area)

Follow the track to the left of the dam which, beyond a cattle-grid, leads along the valley side. After 600 yds (548m), ignore the 'public footpath' sign on the left and continue past Knipe Farm. The track now veers left into the sizeable valley of Mill Clough.

B At the stream the track performs a hairpin, swerving uphill towards the splendidly named Madscar Farm. At the farm entrance, take the track to the left, signposted 'Midshires Way'.

Above the farm the track has been resurfaced near another hairpin which leads up to Overton Hall Farm. Beyond this, continue ahead on the track, still climbing, with fine views to the left across the valley, to arrive at the terminus of Taxal Moor Road at a cattle-grid.

C Follow the finger-post ahead, climbing further across grass, with a plantation on the left, until heather moors are reached. At the crest of the climb there are fine views north-east towards Eccles Pike.

D At a Peak and Northern Footpaths Society cast-iron sign, go half-left for 20 yds (18m), down to a ladder-stile. The path follows the edge of the plantation briefly, then dives into the pines, heading downhill to a boggy hollow crossed by a plank and a strategic log.

A steady rise leads to a stile on the left at the edge of the wood. The path now runs between a wall and the trees before a final short climb.

E Go ahead a few yards beyond the stile to come to the crest of Windgather Rocks. This is a splendid viewpoint west over Cheshire. Head south along the crest of the outcrop, checking for the entertaining activities of rock-climbers. Soon the path comes alongside a minor road.

F Eventually, by a stile on the right, the path goes half-left along a line of posts. If you have started from Pym Chair, simply continue ahead on a concessionary path to return to the car park there.

G If starting the route from the Pym Chair car park, go south on a path as far as the minor road junction. At the information board, turn left. A footpath runs alongside The Street, which rises gently over the ridge. The path along the line of posts (see point **F** above) comes in on the left just to the east of this ridge.

The path continues downhill at the left-hand side of the road, so avoiding the jarring of feet on tarmac. After a mile (1.6km), where a footpath comes in on the left, the path crosses the road, winds briefly among trees, and goes through a broken wall to the top end of the car park. ●

19 Beresford, Wolfscote and Biggin Dales

START Hartington
DISTANCE 5½ miles (8.9km)
TIME 4 hours
PARKING Free in the centre of the village. Also pay-and-display car park at Parsons Field near the public toilets
ROUTE FEATURES Field and riverside paths. Muddy in places. Limestone rocks underfoot are slippery when wet

Beginning in Hartington, this route crosses grassy meadows to reach the River Dove, which is followed through the beautiful Beresford and Wolfscote Dales. Next comes Biggin Dale and a walk on to the limestone plateau, before passing the 17th-century Hartington Hall to complete the circuit.

Hartington is a most attractive place with a market square, a village green and a duck-pond. It became a market town in 1203 and remains busy, mainly catering now for the needs of its many visitors.

From the road sign in the village centre, take the Warslow direction, but only briefly. Between the pottery and public toilets on the left, a footpath leads off. If you start from the Parsons Field car park, this is almost opposite. The footpath has a crushed limestone surface as far as a walled lane, which is crossed via opposing stiles. The path then crosses fields, muddy in places, with several waymarks, on the flank of Pennilow.

Ⓐ At a small gate the path enters woodland. The path drops to the bank of the River Dove, which flows over several weirs.

❓ *According to the plaque, when was this area of woodland planted?*

PUBLIC TRANSPORT Bus connections to Ashbourne, Buxton, Mansfield, Derby and Sheffield. Enquiry line tel. 0870 6082608
REFRESHMENTS Several tearooms and pubs in Hartington
PUBLIC TOILETS Alongside Rooke's Pottery. Passed near start of walk
ORDNANCE SURVEY MAP Outdoor Leisure 24 (The Peak District – White Peak area)

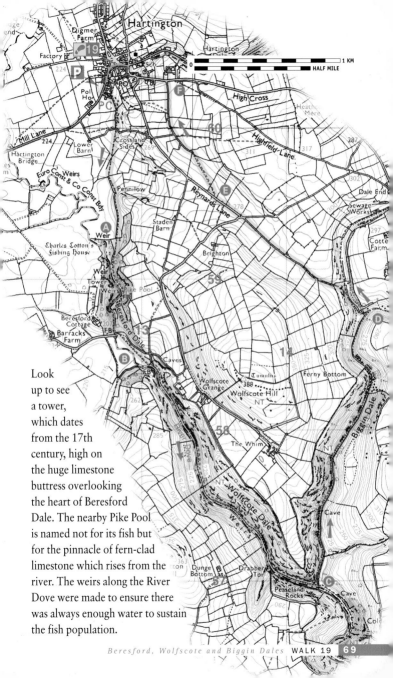

Look up to see a tower, which dates from the 17th century, high on the huge limestone buttress overlooking the heart of Beresford Dale. The nearby Pike Pool is named not for its fish but for the pinnacle of fern-clad limestone which rises from the river. The weirs along the River Dove were made to ensure there was always enough water to sustain the fish population.

Cross to the right riverbank on a wooden footbridge. Before long, there is another footbridge with an ornate stone squeeze-stile alongside it. A flat meadow lies ahead, with the river now on your right again. A path following the wall on the left rises to a stile, from where a track descends back to the valley floor, should the meadow itself be too wet to cross easily.

Hartington village and pond

B Beyond two more stiles, and ignoring yet another footbridge, you enter the narrow confines of Wolfscote Dale. Many limestone outcrops protrude from the slopes of this valley, which is owned by the National Trust.

Of the two crags seen immediately on the left, the nearest one is Frank's Rock. At its base is Frank i' th' Rocks Cave, which has yielded remains from Roman and Anglo-Saxon burials.

A little further south-east, the valley develops a more open aspect with slopes of grass and scree (loose limestone rocks) dotted by a few trees and crags. The river, populated by mallards and the occasional heron, bubbles along over more weirs.

A well-surfaced path runs for most of the valley's length, though from time to time it does get damaged when the river floods. The valley sides begin to lose height gradually before the prominent buttresses of Drabber Tor and Peaseland Rocks appear on the far slope. Ahead, Iron Tors Cave can be seen on the valley side.

C There is no signpost, but where a distinct valley comes in from the left, turn into it immediately before a squeeze-stile in a wall. This is Biggin Dale, which has fewer visitors and a generally wilder appearance than the dales along the Dove.

Biggin Dale is usually a dry valley, only carrying a stream after prolonged rainy spells. Underfoot there are limestone blocks which can be greasy in wet conditions. A short way along on the right is a small cave.

Hartington Hall was built in 1611 in early Jacobean style. It has panelling, mullioned windows and, in one of its rooms, Bonnie Prince Charlie is reputed to have spent the night. For many years now Hartington Hall has been a youth hostel.

At a gate, the Biggin Dale National Nature Reserve begins. The calcareous grassland supports a particularly wide range of wild flowers, which are seen to best effect in summer. The path continues to gain height, paralleling a drystone wall in the valley bottom. Where the wall curves round a dew-pond, follow it to a gate.

D A finger-post showing 'Bridleway to Hartington' points along a tributary valley. After 200 yds (183m), at a further finger-post, the bridleway makes a short, sharp climb to a gate. A walled lane leads ahead, levels out and passes a barn before reaching a junction with a minor road called Reynards Lane.

E Continue ahead for 200 yds (183m) to a wall-stile on the right. Angle half-left across to the far top corner of the field, where the path enters a green lane. This gently loses height before reaching a minor road opposite Hartington Hall youth hostel.

F Turn left, downhill, following the road as it curves right to a junction. Here, turn left for the nearby village centre.

Weir, footbridge and meadow, Beresford Dale

● High peat moorland ● dramatic rock outcrops ● views ● ancient routeway

20 *Kinder Scout and Jacob's Ladder*

This ambitious walk begins near Barber Booth and follows the increasingly wild valley of Crowden Clough to climb to the Kinder Scout plateau. Here is a wonderful 'Dark Peak' landscape with superb views across chocolate-coloured peat and bizarre rock outcrops. A medieval pack-horse trail descending Jacob's Ladder is used to complete the circuit.

START Barber Booth car park

DISTANCE 5½ miles (8.9km)

TIME 4 hours

PARKING Barber Booth car park (free)

ROUTE FEATURES The most ambitious walk in this book. Involves 1,200ft (370m) of ascent. Some easy but avoidable scrambling. Footpaths across fields, rough country, including the rocky banks of a stream (a clough) and high peat moorlands. Often muddy. Dogs must be on a lead

Follow the quiet minor road north-west from the car park to the hamlet of Upper Booth. Immediately beyond the buildings, in the dip where the road crosses a bridge, take the stile on the right indicating a 'Footpath to Open Country'. The path twists and turns above the partly wooded bank of Crowden Brook and climbs a flight of steep retaining steps at one point.

Where the path passes an old barn used to shelter cattle it can be particularly muddy. Half a mile (800m) north of the road, soon after crossing the brook on a one-plank bridge, the path reaches the boundary of open country.

Ⓐ An information board announces that this is the Crowden Clough section of the National Trust's High Peak estate, and illustrates some of the area's typical

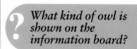

> **?** *What kind of owl is shown on the information board?*

PUBLIC TRANSPORT None suitable

REFRESHMENTS Picnic site at start. Cafés and pubs with outside tables in Edale, 1 mile (1.6km) east

PUBLIC TOILETS Edale

ORDNANCE SURVEY MAP Outdoor Leisure 1 (The Peak District – Dark Peak area)

wildlife. The landscape
steadily takes on a wilder
aspect as the path works its way
up the valley of the Crowden
Brook.

The stream is narrow and its bed
and banks are liberally scattered
with gritstone boulders. At a
couple of points it is necessary to
use the boulders to make easy
stream crossings. As the path gains
height the natural outcrop of
Crowden Tower looms on the
skyline.

The upper part of
the valley provides a chance for
easy and hugely enjoyable
scrambling over layers and shelves
of gritstone. The terrain is such
that you can pick and choose
precisely where you go. Scrambling
can be entirely avoided, if you
prefer not to tackle the rock, by

walking up the steep grassy sides of the valley. This can be awkward if the grass is wet or frosty.

B The gradient relents at the edge of the Kinder Scout plateau, where two streams join to form Crowden Brook. Take the path left for just a few yards to Crowden Tower to enjoy superb views down Crowden Clough and over to the distinctive profile of Mam Tor, 3 miles (4.8km) south-east.

Jacob's Ladder refers to a series of steps cut in this remarkably steep hillside in the 17th century by Jacob Marshall, who lived at Edale Head House, which has now disappeared. The pack-horse bridge, just 27 inches between its low parapets, allowed horses carrying panniers to cross the River Noe at this point. Pack-horses were used in medieval times to carry goods such as coal, salt and wool between Hayfield and the Vale of Edale.

Kinder Scout is what the Dark Peak is all about. The term 'Dark' derives from the colour of both the grit-stone, a type of sandstone that weathers to very dark brown, and the peat. In dry conditions the peat becomes dusty; in wet weather it can be very glutinous! Stay on the path and, although you may get rather peaty, you will not get lost.

Follow the path west beyond Crowden Tower to reach the Wool

The view east across the Wool Packs, Kinder Scout

Packs, a wide area of remarkable rock sculptures protruding from the peat, all the result of natural erosive forces. It is worth exploring the sometimes comical, sometimes brooding outcrops.

Looking up Crowden Clough to Crowden Tower

The path continues further west, gaining height slightly, to Pym Chair **C**, one outcrop among a cluster, then on again to Noe Stool, an isolated boulder. This latter section of the path has been renovated with sandstone flags, making for easier going, especially when the ground is wet.

D From Noe Stool the path trends south-west, with Edale Rocks prominent ahead. On this section a large cairn marks the point where the Pennine Way strikes north.

E Just beyond this cairn, on another stretch with a repaired surface near Swine's Back, the path drops sharply to an obvious track.

F Turn left and quite soon begin the very steep descent of Jacob's Ladder, which twists down to a stone pack-horse bridge. A track now leads on easily to Lee Farm and the adjacent Lee Barn Information Shelter.

G The converted Lee Barn provides seating and information panels explaining the wildlife and ancient trackways of the area.

From here continue along the farm access road to regain the minor road at Upper Booth. The outward route is then followed briefly back to the Barber Booth car park at the starting point. ●

Further Information

Safety on the Hills

The hills, mountains and moorlands of Britain, though of modest height compared with those in many other countries, need to be treated with respect. Friendly and inviting in good weather, they can quickly be transformed into wet, misty, windswept and potentially dangerous areas of wilderness in bad weather. Even on an outwardly fine and settled summer day, conditions can rapidly deteriorate. In winter, of course, the weather can be even more erratic and the hours of daylight are much shorter.

Therefore it is advisable to always take both warm and waterproof clothing, sufficient nourishing food, a hot drink, first-aid kit, torch and whistle. Wear suitable footwear, i.e. strong walking-boots or shoes that give a good grip over rocky terrain and on slippery slopes. Try to obtain a local weather forecast and bear it in mind before you start. Do not be afraid to abandon your proposed route and return to your starting point in the event of a sudden and unexpected deterioration in the weather. Do not go alone. Allow enough time to finish the walk well before nightfall.

Langsett valvehouse

Weir on River Lathkill

Most of the walks described in this book do not venture into remote wilderness areas and will be safe to do, given due care and respect, at any time of year in all but the most unreasonable weather. Indeed, a crisp, fine winter day often provides perfect walking conditions, with firm ground underfoot and a clarity that is not possible to achieve in the other seasons of the year. A few walks, however, are suitable only for reasonably fit and experienced hill walkers able to use a compass and should definitely not be tackled by anyone else during the winter months or in bad weather, especially high winds and mist. These are indicated in the general description that precedes each of the walks.

Follow the Country Code

- Enjoy the countryside and respect its life and work
- Guard against all risk of fire
- Take your litter home
- Fasten all gates
- Help to keep all water clean
- Keep your dogs under control
- Protect wildlife, plants and trees
- Keep to public paths across farmland
- Take special care on country roads
- Leave livestock, crops and machinery alone
- Make no unnecessary noise

- Use gates and stiles to cross fences, hedges and walls
            (The Countryside Agency)

Useful Organisations

Council for National Parks
246 Lavender Hill,
London SW11 1LJ.
Tel. 020 7924 4077

Council for the Protection of Rural England
Warwick House,
25 Buckingham Palace Road,
London SW1W 0PP.
Tel. 020 7976 6433

Countryside Agency
John Dower House,
Crescent Place,
Cheltenham, Gloucs. GL50 3RA.
Tel. 01242 521381

English Heritage
23 Savile Row,
London W1X 1AB.
Tel. 020 7973 3250
www.english-heritage.org.uk

English Nature
Northminster House,
Peterborough, Cambs. PE1 1UA.
Tel. 01733 455100
E-mail: enquiries@english-nature.
org.uk; www.english-nature.org.uk
Heart of England Tourist Board
Larkhill Road,

Worcester WR5 2EZ.
Tel. 01905 761100

National Trust
Membership and general enquiries:
P0 Box 39, Bromley,
Kent BR1 3XL.
Tel. 020 8315 1111
E-mail: enquires@ntrust.org.uk

East Midlands Regional Office:
Clumber Park Stableyard,
Worksop, Notts. S80 3BE.
Tel. 01909 486411

Ordnance Survey
Romsey Road,
Maybush,
Southampton SO16 4GU.
Tel. 08456 05 05 05 (Lo-call)

Peak District National Park
Aldern House, Baslow Road,
Bakewell, Derbyshire DE45 1AE.
Tel. 01629 816200

National Park Authority information centres:
Bakewell, Old Market Hall:
01629 813227
Castleton: 01433 620679
Edale: 01433 670207
Fairholmes: 01433 650953
Hartington (summer weekends, no telephone)
Torside (summer weekends, no telephone)

Ramblers' Association
2nd Floor, Camelford House,
87–90 Albert Embankment,
London SE1 7TW.
Tel. 020 7339 8500

Tourist information centres:
Ashbourne: 01335 343666
Buxton: 01298 25106
Chesterfield: 01246 345777/8
Glossop: 01457 855920
Holmfirth: 01484 222444
Leek: 01538 483 741
Macclesfield: 01625 504114
Matlock: 01629 583388
Matlock Bath: 01629 55082

Youth Hostels Association
8 St Stephen's Hill,
St Albans, Herts. AL1 2DY.

Tel. 01727 855215 (general
enquiries)
Tel. 01727 845047
Tel. 0870 608 2608 (travel line)
E-mail: customerservices@yha.
org.uk

Public transport
(and other transport issues)
With the popularity of the Peak
District and our increasing aware-
ness of the effect of private transport on the environment, you
might wish to consider public
transport as a means of reaching
your walk. For each walk, where
public transport is a possibility,
brief details are given, together
with a telephone contact number
to check current timetables.

Kinder Scout

Recent years have seen a number of new public transport initiatives in the Peak District National Park, together with changes in car-parking arrangements at a number of locations. No doubt things will continue to evolve in this respect during the currency of this book.

Ordnance Survey Maps of the Peak District
Outdoor Leisure maps: 1 (The Peak District – Dark Peak area), 24 (The Peak District – White Peak area)

Answers to Questions:
Walk 1: Tip.

Walk 2: Speedwell Cavern, Treak Cliff Cavern and Blue John Cavern.

Walk 3: Martin Davies.

Walk 4: The Oldham Way.

Walk 5: The Druid Inn.

Walk 6: YHA for Youth Hostels Association.

Walk 7: Alsop, Hartington and Parsley Hay.

Walk 8: 24th May 1989.

Walk 9: A cattle-grid.

Walk 10: The Wriggly Tin Café.

Walk 11: YW, standing for Yorkshire Water.

Walk 12: Red.

Walk 14: Rhodeswood Reservoir.

Walk 15: Victory, Reliance and Royal Soverin [sic].

Walk 16: Whinstone Lee Fields.

Walk 17: Slack Lane.

Walk 19: 1994.

Walk 20: Short-eared owl.